A Cat Slayer

WRITTEN BY MICHÈLE DUFRESNE · ILLUSTRATED BY MAX STASUYK

Pioneer Valley Educational Press, Inc.

One day, Little Knight put on his helmet and his armor and picked up his sword.

"I'm going outside," he told Mother Mouse.

"Be careful," said Mother Mouse. "There are lots of cats outside. Cats like to eat little mice!"

"I am a knight," said Little Knight.
"Knights are brave and strong.
I will slay any cat I see!"

Little Knight went down the road
waving his sword in the air.
"I'm not afraid of any cat," he thought.

He came to a house. There was a picnic table
with presents and a birthday cake.
A piñata was swinging from a tree.
It was big and orange and looked like a cat.
"Aha!" said Little Knight.
"I see a big cat!"

"Beware big cat! I am a knight
and I am going to slay you!" said Little Knight.

Little Knight took out his sword.
SWISH! SWISH!
Candy and toys fell to the ground.

"That is the end of **that** big cat!" he said.
And Little Knight went on down the road.

Little Knight came to a big field.
A little boy was flying a kite.
The kite looked like a cat.
"Aha!" said Little Knight.
"I see a big cat."

The little boy dropped the kite
and ran off to play.

"Beware big cat! I am a knight
and I am going to slay you!" said Little Knight.
Little Knight took out his sword.
SWISH! SWISH!
"That is the end of **that** big cat," he said.
And Little Knight went on down the road.

Next, Little Knight came to a park.
A clown was making animals out of balloons.
He made a dog, a pig, and a cat.
"Aha!" said Little Knight.
"I see a big cat!"

The clown gave
the cat balloon
to a baby.
The baby's mother
put it on top
of the stroller.

The balloon fell to the ground.
Little Knight looked at the cat balloon and said,
"Beware big cat! I am a knight
and I am going to slay you!"

Little Knight took out his sword.
SWISH! SWISH! POP!
"That is the end of **that** big cat,"
said Little Knight.

Little Knight went back home.
"I've had a busy day," he thought.

When he got home his mother asked,
"Did you see any cats?"

"Yes," said Little Knight.
"And I slayed them all!"